ANIMALS

ANIMALS

HUGH WESTRUP & DARREN SECHRIST

Interior Illustrations by Robert Roper

SCHOLASTIC INC.
New York Toronto London Auckland Sydney
Mexico City New Delhi Hong Kong

ISBN 0-439-20410-0

12 11 10 9 8 7   2 3 4 5/0

Printed in the U.S.A.   01

First Scholastic printing, September 2000

CONTENTS

Earth is truly an amazing place. From dogs that have saved their owner's lives to anteaters with tongues that measure up to two feet long, this planet is definitely filled with some strange and interesting creatures! This book will give you more than 100 great facts about all types of animals, from the pets you see every day to prehistoric animals you'll only see in books.

When you're finished reading, we hope that you'll want to either spend hours at the zoo or just watch the animals that are right outside your door! There's a world of wacky creatures out there. Don't you want to *know them all*?

- Fireflies aren't flies; they're beetles. Male fireflies flash their lights while flying through the air. Female fireflies, also called glowworms, don't have wings. They flash their lights on the ground.

- A male praying mantis will try to sneak up on a female praying mantis in order to mate with her. If the female catches a glimpse of the approaching male, she will grab him, pin him down, and eat his head while the two mate.

- Termite colonies build tall mounds, called termitaries, from a material that turns as hard as concrete. If termites were as big as humans, their termitaries would soar to four times the height of New York City's 102-story Empire State Building.

- Fire ants are very warlike. A scientist once watched a war among eighty fire ant colonies that lasted thirty-five days. In the end, only one fire ant colony survived.

- The cockroach is one of Earth's most primitive life-forms. It has roamed the planet pretty much unchanged for 300 million years.

- Mosquitoes eat mainly nectar from flowers.

- Exterminators found fifty thousand killer bees and a honeycomb weighing 210 pounds inside the wall of a house in Tucson, Arizona. The flapping motion of the bees' wings had kept the honey cool and prevented it from melting in the Arizona heat and running all over the floor of the house.

- Bees spread out very far in search of pollen and nectar. If bees were the size of people, a single bee colony would collect pollen and nectar from flowers in an area half the size of Texas.

- Bees are famous for living and working in huge colonies. Believe it or not, though, most of the world's bees live alone in nests in the ground or in holes in trees or buildings.

- Buprestid beetles prefer to mate at the scene of a forest fire. They will fly as far as twenty miles to reach a burning forest.

- The rhinoceros beetle is one of the strongest animals on Earth. It can carry one hundred times its own weight, which

is the same as an adult human carrying approximately five cars.

- The whirligig beetle spends much of its time spinning on the surface of ponds and streams. It has eyes that allow it to see above water and below water at the same time. Half of each eye looks upward and the other half looks downward.

- Snow fleas are tiny insects that live on glaciers and snowbanks and feed on small specks of plant matter.

- In some species of insect, the females can have babies without having to mate with males.

- In Texas and Mexico, water striders are called "Jesus bugs" because they can walk on water.

- Midges are among the smallest flies in the world. They are only about one-twentieth of an inch long. Their small size makes them hard to see, hence their other name: no-see-ums.

- Some young caterpillars increase their weight by four thousand times in just a couple of months. If a newborn human baby grew at the same rate, it would weigh thirteen tons at the end of two months.

- The woolly bear isn't a bear. It's a long-haired type of caterpillar. Woolly bears look cute, but don't pet them, because they produce stinging chemicals.

- The doodlebug digs a pit in the sand by turning its body in backward circles. It then buries itself at the bottom of the pit and waits for small insects to fall into the

pit and into the dooglebug's long, spiny jaws.

- A locust can fly for nine hours without stopping to rest.

- If a locust leg and a human leg were the same size, the locust leg would be one thousand times more powerful.

- Camels can live for up to eight weeks without water. They can do that because they don't sweat much or urinate often. They also store a lot of fat in their humps. The camel combines the oxygen that it breathes with hydrogen in the fat to make water.

- In the mid-1860s, about 13 million bison roamed North America. Twenty years later, human hunters had reduced that number to just a few hundred.

- Pandas are not bears. They belong to their own animal family.

- Don't be surprised if you see a grizzly bear in a vegetarian restaurant. Grizzlies eat mostly plants and some fish.

- The spectacled bear got its name because many have white fur circling both eyes. Those circles make the bears look like they're wearing eyeglasses.

- A grizzly bear can run as fast as a race-horse and much faster than a human Olympic sprinter.

- The duck-billed platypus is one of the few mammals that doesn't have a navel.

- Mongooses aren't birds; they're small mammals that are mainly found in Asia and Africa. Mongooses are able to move very fast and can escape the deadly bite of a snake. Even when bitten by a snake, a mongoose won't die, because snake venom isn't poisonous to it.

- The biggest animal that has ever lived on Earth is the blue whale. An adult blue whale is so huge that an elephant could walk into its opened mouth.

- When two elephants meet, they often twist their trunks together. Such a greeting is called a trunk shake.

- The expression "blind as a bat" isn't true. Bats aren't blind. They see as well as people do. Because bats hunt at night, when insects are most active, they use a kind of radar that lets them know where they are going.

- A zorse is a cross between a horse and a zebra. A zebroid is a cross between a zebra and a donkey.

- An anteater's sticky tongue can be up to two feet long. With each flick of that tongue, the anteater can scoop up as many as five hundred ants.

- An adult panda consumes as much as thirty pounds of bamboo each day. Watching a panda eating a stalk of bamboo is like seeing a pencil going into a pencil sharpener.

- Markhors are a kind of wild goat that have horns shaped like corkscrews.

- Newborn opossums are so tiny that two dozen of them can fit into a teaspoon. They are the size of a grain of rice when they are born, but they triple in size after only one week.

- A hippopotamus named Huberta became a big celebrity in southern Africa when she spent three years traveling one thousand miles from town to town. Huberta was welcome everywhere, though she once had to be scooted out of a movie theater that she had strolled into while a movie was showing.

- Koalas never drink water. The word koala means "no water" in the language of the aboriginal people of Australia.

- Pigs aren't dirty animals. Because their bodies don't sweat, they roll in mud to keep themselves cool. If you gave a pig its own bathtub, it would likely bathe regularly in clean water.

- A wild bear broke into a campground in Canada and ate twenty pounds of dried apples. Later, the bear took a long drink at a nearby creek. The dried apples in the bear's stomach absorbed the water and swelled to their original size, causing the bear to burst and die.

- The dik-dik is a type of antelope that grows to a height of only sixteen inches.

- A baby kangaroo is called a joey. A mother kangaroo is called a flyer. A father kangaroo is called a boomer.

- An elephant produces about fifty pounds of poop every day.

- The okapi is a small, short-necked relative of the giraffe. Okapis use their fourteen-inch-long tongues to clean out their own ears.

- In 1991, an elephant went berserk in India after being bitten on the leg by a king cobra snake. After a twenty-minute rampage, the elephant dropped dead. The cobra died, too, from being trampled by the elephant.

- In 1926, a rainstorm drove millions of mice out of a field and into the town of Taft, California. For weeks and weeks the mice kept on pouring into the town — more than 100 million mice in all. The mice problem finally ended when a large number of birds — hawks, eagles, road-runners, ravens, owls, and gulls — came and attacked the mice.

- The nine-banded armadillo always gives birth to four identical offspring.

- The bald eagle isn't really bald. Its name comes from the old English word *balded*, which means "having white fur or feathers."

- The red-billed oxpecker is a bird that rides on the backs of cattle, picking off ticks and other bugs. The oxpecker gets a tasty meal and the cattle have their backs debugged.

- There are about 100 billion birds living on Earth. Ten billion of those birds are members of a single species, the red-billed quelea.

- Parrots, woodpeckers, and parakeets all have the same type of strange feet. Two of their toes point forward and two point backward.

- An owl doesn't bother picking apart the animals it catches. It eats the animals whole. The parts of an animal that an owl's stomach can't digest are coughed back up in little pellets shaped like hot dogs.

- Hawks travel with the help of warm up-drafts of air called thermals. If a hawk rises a mile on a thermal, it can then glide slowly forward and downward for up to fifteen miles.

- A female pigeon needs to see another pigeon in order to lay eggs, even if she is just seeing herself in a mirror.

- Scottish scientists have found that chickens become calmer, healthier, less aggressive, and lay more eggs when music is piped into their houses.

- The ruffed grouse is a type of bird that goes through a "crazy season" every October. Some ruffed grouse wander into barnyards and act like chickens. Others fly into walls and kill themselves. Still others stroll up to people to have their heads scratched or petted.

- Hanging parrots are tropical birds that hang upside down from the branches of trees. Hanging upside down helps the parrots disguise themselves as leaves.

- A New Zealand woman got the fright of her life when she heard the sound of squawking coming from her oven. The sound was made by a dead chicken that the woman had put into the oven to roast. Steam from the stuffing in the chicken had moved up the bird's neck, where it moved the chicken's vocal cords and caused the bird to squawk.

- Many species of cuckoo bird dump their eggs in the nests of other birds and then take off. After a dumped cuckoo egg hatches, the newborn cuckoo forces all the other young birds out of the nest.

- Crows have been observed throwing nuts in front of oncoming cars. The cars run over the nuts and crush their hard shells. The crows then rush in and eat the nuts.

- Ruby-throated hummingbirds burn a huge amount of energy beating their wings. If an adult man worked as hard as a hummingbird, he would have to eat 238 pounds of hamburger or twice his weight in potatoes each day and produce one hundred pounds of sweat each hour.

- If a high-ranking rooster loses a barnyard fight with a younger rooster, he will run into a corner and hide with his head down and his face to the wall.

- The Baltimore oriole was not named after the city of Baltimore, Maryland. The little black-and-orange bird got its name because its colors are the same as the family colors of Lord Baltimore, the man who established the colony of Maryland in 1632.

- Baby songbirds learn to sing by listening to the adult birds around them. If a baby songbird is put into the nest of another type of songbird family, it will learn the song of its adoptive family.

- The popular dog's name Fido comes from the Latin word *fidus*, which means "loyal."

- A real cat burglar was discovered robbing homes in London. The culprit was a house cat named Tommy that slipped out of the house and stole items such as shoes, designer clothes, and coins, then brought them back to his owner.

- The first year of a dog's life is equal to about twenty-one human years. The remaining years of a dog's life are each equal to about four human years. A ten-year-old dog is fifty-seven in human years.

- Some women in Malaysia raise beautiful butterflies as pets. The women give the butterflies names and wear them as ornaments in their hair.

- The first sky diver was a pet dog. The dog's owner was Jean-Pierre Blanchard, the inventor of the parachute. In 1785,

Blanchard put the dog in a basket tied to a parachute and threw the basket out of a hot-air balloon at a great height. The parachute filled with air, and the basket and dog landed safely on the ground.

- Doug Simpson lost his pet German shepherd, Nick, while vacationing in the Arizona desert. Four months later, Nick showed up, battered and exhausted, at Simpson's house in Selah, Washington, which is more than one thousand miles from where the dog had last been seen.

- In 1692, two pet dogs were tried and hanged for witchcraft in Andover, Massachusetts.

- A pet pig named LuLu saved her owner's bacon. When Jo Ann Altsman suffered a heart attack, LuLu ran out of the house and lay down on the road with her feet in the air. A car stopped and the driver followed LuLu back into the house and called 911. Doctors said that if LuLu hadn't gone for help, Altsman would probably have died.

- Coco, a pet parrot that lived in Syosset, New York, was able to walk the grounds of her owner's home without being attacked by neighborhood cats. Coco could bark like a dog and scare the cats away.

- An average cat sheds about ninety pounds of hair during its lifetime.

- An Irish setter named Lyric saved his master's life with a phone call. Judy Bayly wears a special mask to help her breathe while she sleeps. One night, the mask slipped off her face, causing an alarm to go off. Lyric, remembering his training, ran to the phone and hit a button that dialed 911. Paramedics arrived and saved Bayly.

- When your pet cat rubs the side of his face against you, it may not be because he cares about you. He's marking you with his scent. That mark shows that you are his property and warns other cats to stay away from you.

- U.S. president John Quincy Adams kept an alligator at the White House. President Martin Van Buren had a tiger, and President James Buchanan was the proud owner of an elephant.

- In Diablo, California, a pet cat named Cher spends her days at the local post office, where she likes to lick stamps for customers.

- Ferrets have glands under their tails that give off a foul smell when the animals are scared. Ferrets that are kept as pets have usually had those glands removed.

- U.S. president Franklin D. Roosevelt had a pet dog, Fala, that was almost as famous as he was. A statue of Fala sits next to a statue of his master at the Roosevelt Memorial in Washington, D.C.

- The Westchester Feline Club of New York gave its 1999 Cat of the Year Award to a dog named Ginny. Ginny and her owner, Philip Gonzalez, drive around their neighborhood looking for stray cats.

- Cats have a remarkable ability to survive falls from very high buildings. When a cat's falling body hits a certain speed, the cat can flip itself upright, spread its legs like a parachute, and flatten its body to spread the force of impact. The cat also lands with its legs bent to further absorb the shock.

- The electric eel is not an eel; it is a type of fish called a knifefish. It is just one of five hundred different types of electric fish.

- A female salmon that scientists nicknamed Big Mama returned from the ocean to her native river five times to lay eggs in the river. Most salmon die after laying eggs just once.

- Shovelnose guitarfish are so friendly that people can get free rides by holding on to their tails.

- The lantern shark got its name because it has glands on its body that glow bright green.

- The goby is a small fish that can switch its sex. It can start out as a male, then change into a female, then change back into a male.

- Small fish called wrasses swim inside the mouths of big fish. They do that to pick food from the teeth of the big fish and then eat it.

WE'LL HAVE WHAT YOU'RE HAVING!

- When a flatfish is young, it has an eye on each side of its head. As it gets older, one eye moves to the other side until both eyes are on the same side of the head.

- A female cod lays between 2 million and 9 million eggs at one time. Only about a dozen eggs for every million survive, however. Most of the rest are eaten by other sea creatures.

- The remora fish has a suction fin that it uses to attach itself to other fish and turtles. It then feeds on food that is left over after the other fish or turtle has eaten.

- Turkeyfishes, lionfishes, and stonefishes all have poisonous spines sticking out of their backs. Stonefishes are the deadliest of the three species. Their poison has killed people who have accidentally stepped on them.

- Betta fish, also known as fighting fish, are so aggressive they will attack their own reflection in a mirror.

- Batfish, which have fins that look like bat wings, aren't very good swimmers. Rather than swim, they sometimes use their fins to walk along the bottom of the body of water in which they live.

- Flying fish use their tails to propel themselves out of the water and into the air. They can jump as high as eleven feet out of the water and sail through the air for up to two hundred yards.

- Scientists believe that flying fish jump out of the water to escape their enemies. Once in the air, however, they are often eaten by passing birds.

- A man in Illinois caught a bass that was wearing a pair of glasses over its eyes.

- A starfish pushes its stomach out through its mouth to surround and digest its food.

- Starfish aren't fish. They're echinoderms. An echinoderm is a sea animal that has a spiny skin. Sand dollars, sea urchins, and sea cucumbers are also echinoderms.

- Tiger sharks eat almost anything, it seems. Among the items that have been found in the bellies of tiger sharks are deer antlers, shoes, dogs, a driver's license, a cow's hoof, and a chicken coop with feathers and bones in it.

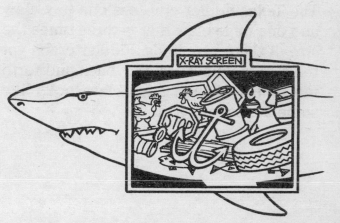

- A mother sea horse puts her eggs in a pouch in the father sea horse's belly. The father carries the eggs there until they hatch.

- The jellyfish is one of the few animals that can change its body size depending on how much food it has to eat. A foot-long jellyfish can shrink to the size of a quarter if food supplies are scarce.

- Hagfish are super slimers. When attacked by a predator, a hagfish squirts a big blob of mucus into the water. The goo clogs the predator's mouth and gills and suffocates it to death.

- The Texas fiddler crab has one tiny claw and one huge claw that is three times the size of the crab's body. Fiddler crabs got their name because the back-and-forth movement of their large claw looks like someone playing a violin.

THE FIDDLER CRAB AT HOME

- A rattlesnake may bite after it's dead. It may bite even after its head has been cut off.

- In 1965, a ferryboat was crossing the crocodile-infested waters of the Shire River, in Africa, when it accidentally flipped over, dumping everyone into the drink. Screams rang out as most of the passengers either drowned or were gobbled up by hungry crocs.

- A rattlesnake once sank its fangs into the tire of a car. Escaping air caused the snake to blow up like a balloon and explode.

- Sea snakes are extremely poisonous. In 1932, a writhing mass of sea snakes that was ten feet wide and seventy-five miles long was spotted in the Strait of Malacca, in Indonesia.

- Some snakes polish their scales using a fluid that comes from their nostrils. At certain times of the year, the snakes polish their scales every day.

- How do frogs and toads differ? The skin of a frog is smooth and moist; the skin of a toad is rough, warty, and dry. Most frogs can live either on land or in water. Toads live in water only during breeding season.

- When a frog is a tadpole it is between seven and ten inches long. As some frogs grow into adulthood they shrink to just two inches or less in length.

- The firebelly toad gives off a poisonous fluid from its skin. The poison doesn't need to make contact with another animal's skin to be irritating. Just smelling it can cause the eyes to burn.

- Many young frogs and salamanders live in vernal pools, which are ponds that appear when spring comes and then dry up by early summer. Vernal pools are safe places for young frogs and salamanders because predatory fish can't survive in them.

- The horned toad is not a toad; it's a lizard. When a horned toad meets an enemy, it shoots blood out of its eyes at the enemy.

- After a female Andean Darwin's frog lays eggs, a group of male frogs divides up the eggs and scoops them into their mouths. The eggs hatch inside the males' mouths and emerge later as tiny frogs.

- The puff adder is an extremely poisonous African snake. Before rifles were invented, hunters tied puff adders to stakes on well-traveled buffalo trails. The angry adders would strike and kill buffalo that came down the trails, and the hunters would eat the dead buffalo.

- Rat snakes sometimes try to eat themselves. A rat snake was once found that had eaten two-thirds of its body.

- A snake can stick out its tongue even when its mouth is closed. It pushes its tongue through a small hole in its upper jaw that is called the lingual fossa.

- How can you tell an alligator from a crocodile? Tell the animal to keep its mouth shut! When an alligator closes its mouth, you can't see any of its teeth. When a crocodile shuts its mouth, a lower tooth sticks out on either side.

- Skunks aren't the only animals that make a stink. Stinkpot turtles release an awful odor whenever they are threatened by an enemy.

- Snakes smell with their tongues. They stick out their tongues to pick up scents in the air. Then they put the tongue into a structure in the mouth that sends a message to the snake's brain.

- A sea snake must come to the surface for air to breathe. Between breaths, however, a sea snake can stay underwater for up to eight hours at a time. It has a lung that takes up most of the space in its body and extends all the way back to its tail.

- A woman named Candelaria Villanueva survived the sinking of a passenger ship six hundred miles off the Philippines. She did it by clinging to the back of a sea turtle, which supported her for two days until she was rescued.

38

- *Titanis* was a species of giant bird that lived in North America several million years ago. It stood more than six feet tall and weighed three hundred pounds. It had a huge beak, powerful arms, and daggerlike claws and preyed on other animals by ambushing them from the tall grass.

- Forty-five million years ago, North America was the home of a creature that some scientists have called the ugliest mammal that has ever lived. Its name was *Uintatherium*, and it had the bulky body of a rhinoceros, two long fangs sticking out from its mouth, and six blunt, bony knobs on its head.

- The quagga was a relative of the zebra that looked as if it had forgotten to put on the bottom half of its striped pajamas. Quaggas lived in southern Africa, and their herds walked in single file across the plains in search of food.

- Giants birds called moa once lived on the islands of New Zealand. Some moa were as small as turkeys, but the largest ones were twelve feet tall and weighed half a ton. Moa were hunted to extinction by human beings several hundred years ago.

- Marsupials are mammals that carry their babies in pouches. Most marsupials, such as the kangaroo, live in Australia. One prehistoric marsupial, *Diprotodon*, was as big as a hippopotamus.

- The longest living snake on record was a reticulated python that measured thirty-three feet. A prehistoric species of snake called *Gigantophis* lived 60 millon years ago and grew to sixty-five feet long.

- The biggest meat-eating mammal that ever lived was a fierce, doglike creature that inhabited Asia 35 million years ago. Called *Andrewsarchus*, it was sixteen feet long and weighed close to a ton. It belonged to a family of mammals, some of whose members evolved into whales.

- A hooved animal called *Synthetoceras* lived in North America millions of years ago. It had a big Y-shaped horn on its nose that would have made a great slingshot. The males probably used their horns in fights to determine which was the most powerful male in a herd.

- *Platybelodon* was a prehistoric elephant that lived in North America and had a five-foot-long lower jaw shaped like a huge shovel. At the end of its jaw were two big flat teeth. Some scientists think the "shovel tusker" used its two big teeth to scrape the bark and strip the leaves off trees.

- *Pterichthyodes* was a little fish that lived about 370 million years ago. It was built like an armored truck. It had bony plates covering the front of its body and tough scales covering the back.

- Many people think spiders are insects, but they're not. They're arachnids. Insects have three body parts and six legs; arachnids have two body parts and eight legs. Insects have antennae; arachnids don't. Mites, ticks, and scorpions are also arachnids.

- Male black widow spiders have to be very careful when they mate with female black widow spiders. If a male approaches a female in the wrong way, she may mistake him for an enemy and kill and eat him.

- The centipede is an animal whose name means "one hundred feet." A centipede can have anywhere from twenty-eight to 354 legs, however, depending on which species it belongs to.

- Your bed contains millions of tiny arachnids called dust mites. Dust mites can only be seen under a microscope. Dust mites feed on the dead skin cells that the human body sheds in bed. Beds are also nice for mites because the warmth and sweat produced by a sleeping body keeps the little arachnids comfy and moist.

- Many people think the daddy longlegs is a spider, but it's not. It is part of the same family as the spider (the arachnids) but is different because it has only one body segment, while all spiders have two. Also, it has eight legs like the spider but does not spin webs like spiders do.

- Scorpions can survive for more than a year without food. They can also live for fifteen to twenty-five years — longer than any other known arachnid or insect.

- Water spiders in Europe and Asia live underwater in small, air-filled tents. To refill the air in a tent, a water spider occasionally swims to the surface and captures tiny air bubbles between the hairs on its legs and abdomen.

- A female tick can suck enough blood in just two days to grow up to two hundred times her original weight.

- Tarantulas look scary, but their bite is less painful and less dangerous than the sting of a bee.

- The teensy-weensy male Nephila orb-weaving spider weighs one thousand times less than the female. He can walk all over her without even attracting her attention.

- Demodex is a mite that, under a microscope, looks like a tiny crocodile; it lives in human eyelashes and eyebrows. Almost every person has a large colony living on his or her face.

- The female bola spider "fishes" for her victims. She lures male moths by producing the scent of a female moth. When a male moth approaches, the female spider casts out a long, sticky "fishing" line and swings it toward the moth. If the line hits its target, the spider reels in the moth and has lunch.

- Earthworms crawl onto sidewalks during a rainstorm because their holes fill with water. If they didn't come outside, they would drown.

- Roving entertainers in West Africa keep large poisonous scorpions as pets. They let the scorpions live in their clothing and train the scorpions to do tricks.

Hugh Westrup is the editor of *Current Science*, a children's classroom magazine. He has written several books, including *Prehistoric North America: The Mammals; Maurice Strong: Working for Planet Earth;* and *Bite Size Science, Bite Size Geography, Bite Size History,* and *Bite Size Biography.* He lives in New York City.

Darren Sechrist lives in Connecticut with his wife, Jenne, and their cat, Peaches. During the day, Darren designs educational software for children. In his spare time, he performs stand-up comedy in New York City.